No Wheat? No Way!

Gluten-Free Recipes You've Been Waiting For

Kid Approved
Milk Free

Theresa Santandrea-Cull

Well Street Publications Inc.

For my Dad

National Library of Canada Cataloguing in Publication

Santandrea-Cull, Theresa, 1958-
   No wheat? No way! : Gluten-free Recipes You've Been Waiting
For / Theresa Sanandrea-Cull.

Includes index.
ISBN 0-9731752-0-6

   1. Wheat-free diet—Recipes. 2. Gluten-free diet—Recipes.
3. Milk-free diet—Recipes. I. Title.

RM237.86.S25 2003   641.5'63   C2003-906463-8

Printed in Canada.

To order books, please contact
Hushion House Publishing Limited
36 Northline Road
Toronto, Ontario M4B 3E2, Canada
Telephone 1-416-285-6100
Fax 1-416-285-1777

**Dedicated to my twin boys,
Eli and Joseph.**

This book was inspired as a result of my children's gluten
and dairy intolerance. I thank God for them and the
health care practitioners who diagnosed their condition.

If you are reading this book perhaps you or
a loved one is affected by the same intolerance.
Don't give up, this book will help you as it did my family.
We all feel better for it.

Enjoy!

Theresa Santandrea-Cull

Table of Contents

Brownies, Cookies, Frosting, Icing, Pudding, and Squares

Cobbler, Fruit Crisps, Pies, and Tarts

Main Dishes, Sauces, and Side Dishes

Foreword

Well, you've received the news, NO GLUTENS, NO DAIRY! from your health care practitioner, now what? "What am I going to do without breads and muffins and dairy products, ahhhh! No more desserts?" No need to worry a bit longer. No Wheat? No Way! Gluten-Free Recipes You've Been Waiting For is your ticket to delightful eating and delicious indulgences.

Millions of ill-advised people continue to suffer needlessly from a variety of disorders directly linked to food allergies and intolerance. It is estimated that 80% of our diseases are directly linked to the foods we consume on a daily basis. Imagine being free of all your joint pain just by avoiding those foods to which you are intolerant. Anyone can attain better health by identifying, then avoiding their particular food allergens. The most common food allergens are the Dairy Products and Gluten Grains. Now avoiding these allergic foods is a process, which all seem to agree, requires considerable help.

As one might expect, this is a multifaceted challenge that requires flexibility, dedication, support and resources. This cookbook is a wonderful resource for anyone wanting to make that change towards a non-gluten, non-dairy lifestyle. This book has been tailored to support the reader in a fun and decadent way, one that is not far from our cultural experiences. Just like mom's home cooking!

Theresa Santandrea-Cull has done a terrific job bringing to us the joys of desserts while avoiding those common allergens most of us should avoid in keeping with a healthy diet. May you enjoy these delicious desserts and main dishes in the very best of health.

The key to improving one's diet is learning how to prepare more nutritious foods, deliciously!

Dawn Cormier-Hazen, N.D.
President of Sunrise Health Services Inc.

Secret Information

Alternative To Baking Powder

All recipes call for gluten-free baking powder and sodas. Use your own or the following:

In a large bowl, sift together:

$1/4$ cup baking soda
$1/4$ cup cream of tartar
$1/4$ cup potato starch flour

Mix thoroughly and keep in a tightly covered jar or container. When a recipe calls for baking powder, use the equivalent amount of your new alternative baking powder. To check if mixture is still active, add a few drops of water. If it bubbles vigorously, it is still good.

Alternative to Chocolate

Carob can be substituted for chocolate.

1 cup chocolate chips	=	1 cup sweetened carob chips
1 cup chocolate chips	=	$1/2$ cup unsweetened carob chips + $1/4$ - $1/2$ cup raw sugar
1 ounce square of chocolate	=	3 tablespoons carob powder + 2 tablespoons dairy free milk

Semi-Sweet Chocolate Chips

I always use semi-sweet chocolate chips, as most brands do not contain milk. Check your grocery store or alternative health food store to see what products they carry.

Alternatives to White Sugar

Brown Sugar

1 packed tablespoon brown sugar	=	1 tablespoon granulated white sugar

Raw Sugar

1 tablespoon raw sugar	=	1 tablespoon granulated white sugar

Sucanat (sugar cane natural)

1 tablespoon Sucanat	=	1 tablespoon granulated white sugar

Turbinado Sugar

1 tablespoon turbinado sugar	=	1 tablespoon granulated white sugar

Kitchen Conversion

3 teaspoons	=	15 ml	=	1 tablespoon
4 teaspoons	=	60 ml	=	1/4 cup
5 1/3 tablespoons	=	79 ml	=	1/3 cup
8 tablespoons	=	118 ml	=	1/2 cup
16 tablespoons	=	237 ml	=	1 cup
1 fl. oz	=	30 ml	=	2 tablespoons
8 fl. oz	=	237 ml	=	1 cup
16 fl. oz	=	473 ml	=	2 cups or 1 pint
32 fl. oz	=	946 ml	=	4 cups or 1 quart

Dry Measure

0.035 oz	=	1.00 gram
1 oz	=	28.35 grams
1 lb	=	453.59 g or 0.45 kg
2.21 lbs	=	1.00 kilograms

Variables

Egg Size:
   I use large Omega 3 eggs.

Cookie Tray:
   I use a nonstick cookie sheet.

Sugar:
   I have used turbinado sugar and raw sugar in all my recipes.

Dairy Free Milk:
   All recipes have been made with rice milk.

Gluten-free flours:
   All recipes have been made with Bob's Red Mill® gluten-free flour and/or Health food stores' gluten-free flours.

All recipes call for gluten-free products.

Breads, Loaves, Pancakes, and Other Breakfast Delights

Banana Bread

This recipe is truly crowd pleasing.

In a large bowl, combine the following:

 $3/4$ cup white rice flour
 $1/3$ cup potato starch flour
 $1/2$ cup chopped hazelnuts
 2 teaspoons baking powder
 1 teaspoon salt
 $1/4$ teaspoon baking soda

In another large bowl, cream together:

 $1/3$ cup softened butter
 $1/2$ cup raw sugar

Now, beat in:

 2 eggs
 1 cup mashed bananas

Pour liquid ingredients into flour mixture, stir only until flour is moistened. Pour batter into a greased loaf pan. Bake at 350°F for 50-60 minutes.

Banana Scones

Simply marvelous. Our friend Jake wanted this for his birthday cake. How could I refuse. He turned 6 years old this year. Happy Birthday Jake.

In a large bowl, stir together:

> 1 1/2 cups brown rice flour
> 1/4 cup white rice flour
> 1/2 cup raw sugar
> 2 teaspoons baking powder
> 1/2 teaspoon salt
> 1/4 teaspoon baking soda

Then cut in with a pastry blender until crumbly, and set aside:

> 4 tablespoons cold butter

In another bowl, mix together:

> 2 eggs
> 1 cup mashed bananas
> 1/2 cup rice milk
> 1 teaspoon vanilla

Add the dry ingredients to the wet until just combined. Pour onto a greased 9" round pizza pan, to form a round mound of batter.

Sprinkle the top with:

> 1/3 cup chopped hazelnuts
> 2 tablespoons raw sugar

Bake at 400°F for 20 minutes. Cut into 8-10 sections and serve.

Banana and Strawberry Shake

This is a good recipe to use when you need to get rid of those ripe bananas sitting on the counter.

In a blender, add:

> 2 bananas
> 8 strawberries
> 1-2 cups rice milk (or your preference)

You may add any type of dairy free milk depending on which you and your children prefer. My children can't tell the difference, so I use whichever I have on hand. If you prefer a thicker shake, use less milk and visa versa.

Blend at high speed for 1 minute. Pour into 2 large glasses, add a straw, a strawberry and a slice of orange on the top of the glass just for fun. Your children will love you forever.

You may use any combination of fruit. I've used them all. This is our favourite. Just make sure to always add a banana to give the thickness of a milkshake.

In the summer, I like to make this recipe into frozen treats. The kids love them.

Bread

One of the very best investments I made was my bread maker. I couldn't achieve the same results without it. It has been my saving grace. And if you haven't had bread for awhile this is pure heaven.

Using a bread maker, place the following ingredients in order, in bread pan:

1 1/2 cups rice milk
3 eggs
4 tablespoons honey
2 teaspoons salt
4 tablespoons softened butter
2 cups white rice flour
1 1/2 cups tapioca flour
1 1/2 cups potato starch flour
1 1/2 teaspoons dry active yeast

Select dough setting and start. After the first kneading time, remove pan and pour dough into two greased bread pans. Let rise in warm oven for 45 minutes to 1 hour. Bake at 350°F for 20 minutes, or until your knife comes out clean.

This bread is delicious warm, with butter and strawberry jam, ...mmmmm good. I served this to a client with a cup of tea. He thought he was in seventh heaven. I've been baking it ever since.

If you choose to make rice flour bread, it is best to keep it in the refrigerator. (It will stay fresh longer.) Or you may choose to slice it, and then place it in the freezer and use it as you need it (making sure to toast it when you do.) Usually, by the next day, I have only one or two slices left. I find that this is an ideal time to make French Toast in the morning for breakfast; what better way to start the day!

Cinnamon Buns

These buns are a little time consuming, but well worth the effort. Eli, Joseph and their friends gobble them up so fast that I have to make two batches!

In a large bowl, combine the following with a pastry blender until crumbly:

1 1/2 cups white rice flour   1 teaspoon salt
1/2 cup tapioca flour   1/4 cup cold butter
4 teaspoons baking powder

In a measuring cup, beat slightly:

1 egg

Add vanilla dairy free milk to measure 1 cup.

Add your egg mixture to the flour mixture to form a soft dough. Place your dough on a floured piece of wax paper measuring 12 inches long. Sprinkle the dough lightly and evenly with rice flour and place a second sheet of wax paper on top of the floured dough. Take your rolling pin and roll out dough to make a rectangular shape, about 12 inches long. Set aside.

Filling

In another bowl, cream together:

1/3 cup softened butter   3 teaspoons cinnamon
1/2 cup raw sugar

Remove the top sheet of wax paper and spread the filling evenly over dough. Carefully roll dough removing the bottom sheet of wax paper as you roll. Using a serrated knife, cut into 12 pieces. Place cut side down into a greased muffin tin. Bake at 350°F for 12-15 minutes.

Icing

In a small bowl, stir together:

1/4 cup fruit powdered sugar   1 tablespoon dairy free milk

Drizzle over warm cinnamon buns. Ahhhh....

Cranberry and Banana Loaf

This is my family's all time favourite. It never lasts longer than a day.

In a large bowl, combine until blended:

$3/4$ cup white rice flour
$1/4$ cup brown rice flour
2 teaspoons baking powder
$1/4$ teaspoon salt
$1/2$ teaspoon cinnamon

In another large bowl, cream together:

$1/4$ cup softened butter
$1/2$ cup raw sugar

Then whip in:

2 eggs
2 small ripe bananas (mashed with a fork)
1 cup frozen cranberries

Add the dry ingredients to the wet, and stir until moistened. Pour into greased loaf pan. Bake at 350°F for about 45 minutes. You may want to check your loaf at 35 minutes because, as you know, rice flour is finicky.

Crépes Anyone?

In a large bowl, mix until well combined:

$1/2$ cup brown rice flour
$1/4$ cup tapioca flour
$1/4$ cup potato starch flour
$1/2$ teaspoon salt
2 eggs
$1/2$ cup plain rice milk
$1/2$ teaspoon raw sugar
$1/2$ teaspoon vanilla

In a medium size frying pan, add a teaspoon of butter. When pan is hot, add a $1/8$ cup of crépe batter and swerve the pan around to make a nice size crépe (remember, thin is the key). When edges start to lift, flip the crépe over and cook the other side about 1 minute. Place on side dish and cook another and another and another, until the batter is all gone.

Filling

Thaw one 250 gram package of frozen blueberries (fresh 1 cup), or strawberries, or why not be daring and use $1/2$ cup of each — fantastic! Add berries to sauce pan with 2 table-spoons of Torani® Original Italian Syrup; blueberry flavour found at specialty coffee shops.Add 1 tablespoon of potato starch flour and stir constantly over medium heat until it comes to a boil. Pour over individual crépes and roll. Sprinkle with fruit sugar and serve. Your children will adore you.

French Toast

I discovered this recipe when I was completely out of bread. These rice cakes turned out nicely, and they are very tasty.

In a large flat bottom bowl, beat well the following ingredients:

> 1 egg
> 1/4 cup dairy free milk
> 1 teaspoon vanilla

Place plain rice cake in egg mixture and let stand 3-5 minutes.

Place a teaspoon of butter in frying pan, add rice cake and cook as usual.

Sprinkle with a little cinnamon and maple syrup. Voilà, French Toast.

Fretella

Pancakes Italian Style for Pancake Tuesday. Thanks Mom.

In a large bowl, stir to combine:

    1 cup white rice flour
    2 teaspoons baking powder
    1 tablespoon raw sugar
    dash salt

Then add the following and stir until just moistened:

    2 eggs
    1 tablespoon grated lemon rind
    juice from same lemon
    1 cup rice milk

Pour dollops (size of 1 tablespoon) of batter, in a hot frying pan with 1 inch of hot vegetable oil. Turn over when edges are slightly brown. Cook 1 minute more and remove to paper towel to absorb some of the oil. Place on serving dish and sprinkle with fruit sugar powder. Serve hot to warm. Use at supper time on Pancake Tuesdays.

Hazelnut Crépes

In a large bowl, whisk together until smooth:

 1/2 cup brown rice flour
 1/4 cup tapioca flour
 1/4 cup potato starch flour
 1/4 cup hazelnut cocoa powder
 pinch of salt
 1 tablespoon melted butter
 2 eggs
 1 cup dairy free milk

Pour 1/4 cup of batter into slightly buttered nonstick pan. Cook over medium heat for about 1 minute, then flip and cook the other side slightly.

There you have it, a beautiful Hazelnut Crépe. Sprinkle with sliced strawberries and roll. Don't forget to add the maple syrup. Pure heaven.

Lemon Poppy Seed Loaf

This is our friend Ivan's favourite cake. He was amazed to find out that it was baked with rice flour.

In a large bowl, mix the following ingredients:

 1 1/4 cups white rice flour
 1 tablespoon poppy seeds
 2 teaspoons baking powder

In another large bowl, cream together until fluffy:

 1/2 cup raw sugar
 1/3 cup softened butter

Then add:

 1 egg
 1 grated lemon rind
 3 tablespoons lemon juice from the same lemon
 1/3 cup plain rice milk

Add dry ingredients to wet until just combined. Pour into a greased loaf pan. Bake at 350°F for 40 minutes or until knife comes out clean or toothpick, whichever you prefer.

Glaze

While your loaf is baking, stir together:

 1/8 cup raw sugar
 2 tablespoons lemon juice (from the same lemon as above)

Let lemon loaf sit for at least 10 minutes before attempting to remove it from the loaf pan. Poke holes into the baked loaf with a toothpick and pour glaze over the top. Place on a beautiful serving dish and serve your friends this beautiful lemon loaf with your favourite blend of tea.

Pancakes

In a large bowl, mix together until smooth:

   1/2 cup white rice flour
   1/2 cup brown rice flour
   1 teaspoon baking powder
   1/4 teaspoon baking soda
   1/4 teaspoon salt
   1 teaspoon vanilla
   2 teaspoons vegetable oil
   1 teaspoon maple syrup (I sometimes add 2)
   1 egg
   1 cup dairy free milk

Add more milk if necessary, until you get a fairly thin batter. Place two pats of butter in a hot nonstick frying pan. Add a 1/4 cup of batter or less, depending on desired size of pancake. Flip pancake when batter starts to bubble and continue cooking other side for another minute. Place two pancakes on a plate, top it with berries, add a little maple syrup. You now have a very nutritious breakfast. Enjoy!

Variations:

   Add 1/2 cup of fresh or frozen blueberries to finished batter and stir in gently.
   or Add 1/2 cup applesauce with a 1/4 teaspoon cinnamon.
   or Add 1/2 cup pearsauce with a 1/4 teaspoon cinnamon.
   or Add 1/2 cup banana purée.

Note:

I sometimes double the recipe using the dry ingredients only. I then label my container "Pancake Mix" and store it in the cupboard until next time. Remembering to use only half of the doubled recipe, I then follow the remaining recipe.

Popovers

(or Yorkshire Pudding)

These will compliment any meal when you need a bread or crave one for that matter. I love to bake them when we eat soup.

In a large bowl, stir after each ingredient:

1 cup dairy free milk
1/2 cup white rice flour
2 eggs
1/4 teaspoon salt
1 tablespoon melted butter

Pour the popover batter evenly into a greased muffin tin for 12. Bake at 450°F for 15 minutes, then reduce heat to 350°F and bake for another 5-8 minutes. These are absolutely fantastic!

Tea Biscuits

These are the best!

In a large bowl, mix thoroughly the following:

> 1 cup brown rice flour
> 1/4 cup tapioca flour
> 1/4 cup potato starch flour
> 4 teaspoons baking powder
> 1/2 teaspoon salt

Cut in with a pastry blender until crumbly:

> 1/3 cup butter

Pour in:

> 1 cup dairy free milk

Stir until just combined. Let dough sit for 5 minutes. Using 1/4 cup measuring cup, scoop out a 1/4 cup for each serving and place it on a cookie sheet. Bake at 350°F for about 8-10 minutes. Let tea biscuits cool on cookie rack. Then add butter and strawberry jam and you are in heaven.

Waffles

My waffle maker was the other best investment I made. If you can, buy one when they are on sale. You'll never regret it. I like to make a whole batch of waffles and toast the leftovers the next day. Who knew heaven could be found in such simple pleasures.

In a large bowl, mix together the following ingredients:

1 $1/4$ cups white rice flour
$1/4$ cup potato starch flour
1 tablespoon baking powder
$1/2$ teaspoon salt

Then stir in until well blended, these ingredients:

2 cups dairy free milk
2 egg yolks
$1/3$ cup vegetable oil

Now, in another bowl, beat until stiff:

2 egg whites.

Slowly fold egg whites into batter. Scoop batter with a $3/4$ cup measurer, and pour it onto the hot griddle. Bake 3-5 minutes or until steam stops. Repeat with remaining batter and serve with your favourite fruit.

Cakes
and
Muffins

Angel Food Cake

This is my traditional birthday cake for my boys. But you don't have to wait for birthdays to make this beautiful cake.

In a small bowl, stir together then set aside:

> 1 cup white rice flour
> 3/4 cup raw sugar

In a very large bowl, beat until stiff:

> 14 egg whites
> 1 1/4 teaspoons cream of tartar

Gradually add 3/4 cup raw sugar, while beating egg whites for about 2-3 minutes.

Fold flour mixture into egg white bowl, then pour batter into lightly floured angel food cake pan. Bake at 350°F for 30 minutes.

Variations:

For a chocolate taste, grate 1/2 cup semi-sweet chocolate and fold it into the egg white mixture with flour.

Icing

In a saucepan, melt 3/4 cup of semi-sweet chocolate chips with a 1/4 cup of dairy free milk until smooth. Pour over cooled angel food cake and top with sliced strawberries. Yummy!

Apple Streusel Coffee Cake

My husband Andrew, prefers sliced peaches to apples, and I love this cake both ways. Experiment and have fun.

Topping

In a very small bowl, cream together and set aside:

1/4 cup raw sugar
2 tablespoons rice flour
1 teaspoon cinnamon
2 tablespoons softened butter

Batter

In a medium size bowl, stir these dry ingredients together:

1 cup rice flour
2 teaspoons baking powder
1/2 teaspoon salt

Now cream together the following in a large bowl:

1/3 cup softened butter
1/4 cup raw sugar

Stir in:

1 egg

Then add:

3/4 cup dairy free milk

Add the dry ingredients to the wet ingredients, and stir until just combined. Pour batter into a greased round cake pan. Sprinkle topping evenly over batter. Now add thin slices of apples and place on top. Bake at 350°F for 25-30 minutes. Serve with coffee for breakfast or serve it to your friends for a coffee social. They will be pleasantly surprised.

Banana Chocolate Chip Muffins

Do you love chocolate as much as we do?

In a small bowl, combine the following:

> 1 cup white rice flour
> 3 teaspoons baking powder
> 1 cup semi-sweet chocolate chips (dairy free)

In a large bowl, whip together:

> 1/3 cup softened butter
> 1/3 cup raw sugar

Then add, beating well:

> 2 eggs
> 2-3 small mashed bananas measuring, 1 cup
> 2 teaspoons vanilla

Add dry ingredients to wet. Stir until just blended. Scoop into buttered muffin tins, about 3/4 full. Bake at 350°F for 15-20 minutes. Let stand 5 minutes before removing from muffin tin. This recipe makes about 12 muffins.

Blueberry Upside Down Cake

I love blueberries! This is one of my favourites.

Over low heat, in a saucepan, stir the following ingredients:

> 2 cups blueberries
> 1 tablespoon raw sugar
> 1 tablespoon rice flour

Bring this to a boil and pour into a buttered 8 inch cake pan. Set aside.

In a bowl, combine the following:

> 1 1/2 cups white rice flour
> 2 teaspoons baking powder
> 1/4 teaspoon salt

In another bowl, cream together:

> 1/2 cup raw sugar
> 1/4 cup softened butter

Stir in:

> 1 egg
> 2 teaspoons grated lemon rind
> 1 cup dairy free milk

Beat until smooth. Add the dry ingredients to the wet and stir until just combined. Pour batter evenly over blueberries. Bake at 350°F for 20-25 minutes. Let cool 5-10 minutes before attempting to turn cake over. Cut into squares. For a little pizzazz, sprinkle it with fruit sugar. Enjoy!

Carrot and Pineapple Muffins

After awhile you'll think that "Betty Crocker" had visited your home. These are great. Between the four of us, there is never any left for the next day.

In a large bowl, combine and set aside:

   3/4 cup brown rice flour
   1/2 cup tapioca flour
   1/2 cup raw sugar
   2 teaspoons baking powder
   1/2 teaspoon salt
   1 teaspoon cinnamon

In another large bowl, whip together:

   2 eggs
   1 cup grated carrot
   1 cup crushed unsweetened pineapple

Add the dry ingredients to the wet ingredients and stir just until moist. Pour into greased muffin tin. Bake at 350°F for 15-20 minutes. Let the muffins stand for 5 minutes before removing them from the muffin tin. Cool on a cookie rack before serving.

Cinnamon Pear Muffins

Everyone will be sinfully delighted. When entertaining, you may want to make the muffins in petite muffin tins — just make sure you reduce your cooking time.

In a large bowl, combine the following ingredients:

1 cup brown rice flour	3 teaspoons baking powder
1/2 cup tapioca flour	1 teaspoon salt
1/2 cup potato starch flour	1 teaspoon cinnamon
1/2 cup raw sugar	

In another bowl, cream together:

1/2 cup raw sugar	2/3 cup softened butter

Then add, beating well:

2 eggs
2/3 cup dairy free milk (your choice)
1 cup grated pear or pearsauce

Add the dry ingredients to the wet, and stir until moistened. Spoon into greased muffin tins. Bake at 350°F for 12-15 minutes or until your butter knife comes out clean. Wait 5 minutes, before removing from your muffin tin. Add the glaze from the following recipe to make the muffins more festive.

Glaze

Take out two small bowls. In one bowl, add:

2 tablespoons melted butter

In the other bowl, mix together:

1/2 teaspoon cinnamon	1/4 cup raw sugar

When your muffins are warm, dip one muffin into the melted butter bowl, then swirl the same muffin into the cinnamon and sugar bowl. Let cool on muffin rack. Repeat for the remaining muffins.

Fabulous Coffee Cake

Warning! You will need three bowls.

Topping

In a small bowl, combine until crumbly and set aside:

  1 cup ground hazelnuts or ground pecans
  $1/4$ cup raw sugar
  $1/2$ teaspoon cinnamon
  $1/4$ teaspoon nutmeg
  pinch of cloves
  3 tablespoons softened butter

In another small bowl, combine the following and set aside:

  1 cup white rice flour
  2 teaspoons baking powder
  $1/2$ teaspoon salt

In a large bowl, cream together:

  $1/3$ cup raw sugar
  2 tablespoons softened butter

Stir in:

  1 egg
  1 teaspoon vanilla

Next, stir in slowly:

  $2/3$ cup plain dairy free milk

Gradually stir flour mixture into the milk mixture, until just wet. Pour half the batter into an 8 inch round cake pan. Sprinkle with half the topping. Add the remainder of the batter and finish with the topping. Bake at 350°F for 20-25 minutes. Absolutely fabulous, hence the name of the cake. This is our friend Frank's favourite.

Fast and Easy Chocolate Cake

In a saucepan, over low heat, stirring constantly until smooth, add:

$1/2$ cup butter
$1/3$ cup unsweetened cocoa powder

Remove from heat.

In a large bowl, combine:

$1/2$ cup raw sugar
$1/2$ cup white rice flour
2 teaspoons baking powder
$1/4$ teaspoon salt

In another large bowl, whisk together:

2 eggs

Then add:

$1/2$ cup dairy free milk
1 teaspoon vanilla

Now add the chocolate from the saucepan to the egg mixture. Stir. Add the flour mixture and stir again until combined. Pour into a greased 8 inch cake pan. Bake at 350°F for 30 minutes. Let cool for 10 minutes before attempting to remove from cake pan. Frost with Chocolate Icing found on page 54. Yummy!

Substitutions:

carob powder for cocoa powder

Mom's Cake

My Mom's cake is the best cake ever; everyone loves it. But if you can't have the real thing, this recipe is the next best thing. Enjoy!

In a large bowl, sift together:

> 2 cups white rice flour
> 2 teaspoons baking powder

In another large bowl, cream together until nice and fluffy:

> 1/2 cup softened butter
> 3/4 cup raw sugar

Then whisk in:

> 4 eggs
> 2 teaspoons vanilla

Gently stir in:

> 1 cup rice milk

Add the dry ingredients slowly to the wet ingredients, stirring until just moistened. Pour into a greased angel food cake pan. Sprinkle with raw sugar. Bake at 350°F for 30-40 minutes.

Thanksgiving Cake

I serve this cake at every Thanksgiving meal and we all enjoy it every time. It's moist and fabulous.

In a large bowl, combine the following:

3/4 cup white rice flour
3/4 cup brown rice flour
2 1/2 teaspoons baking powder
1/4 teaspoon salt
1 teaspoon ginger
1 teaspoon cinnamon
1/2 teaspoon nutmeg
1/2 teaspoon allspice

In another bowl, cream together:

1/2 cup softened butter
1/2 cup raw sugar

Stir in:

3 eggs
1/2 cup fancy molasses
3/4 cup dairy free milk

Slowly add the dry ingredients to the wet ingredients until just combined. Pour into a greased cake pan and sprinkle the top with raw sugar. Bake at 350°F for 20-25 minutes. Let sit for 10 minutes before removing from pan. Serve to your guests hot or cold with a scoop of vanilla soya milk ice cream. Ahhh...

White Cake

Joseph says,"It's amazing, two thumbs up!"

In a small bowl, combine the following then set aside:

   1 cup white rice flour
   2 tablespoons baking powder
   1/2 teaspoon salt

In a large bowl, cream together:

   1/2 cup softened butter
   1/2 cup raw sugar

Add, then set aside:

   3 egg yolks
   1 teaspoon vanilla
   1/2 cup dairy free milk

In another bowl, beat until stiff:

   3 egg whites

Stir the dry ingredients with the wet to make a batter. Then, gently fold the egg whites into batter, maybe 3 times . Pour into two greased cake pans. Bake at 350°F for 15-20 minutes. Let cool before attempting to remove from cake pans. Frost the top of one cake, then gently place the second cake, bottom side up, on the first. Frost the top and sides with a white or chocolate frosting.

Zucchini Muffins

In a large bowl, stir together:

    1 1/2 cups brown rice flour
    1 1/2 teaspoons baking powder
    1/2 teaspoon baking soda
    1 1/2 teaspoons cinnamon
    1/2 teaspoon salt

In another large bowl, cream together:

    1/4 cup softened butter
    1/2 cup raw sugar

Then stir in:

    1 egg
    1/2 cup dairy free milk
    1 cup grated zucchini

Add the dry ingredients to the wet, and stir until just combined. Pour into greased muffin tins, 3/4 full. Bake at 400°F for 20-25 minutes. Add glaze if desired, from Cinnamon Pear Muffins recipe found on page 36.

Substitutions for zucchini:

    1 cup bananas
    1 cup cranberries
    or 1/2 cup of each

Brownies, Cookies, Frosting, Icing, Pudding and Squares

Applesauce Cookies

In a small bowl, combine:

>   1 1/2 cups brown rice flour
>   2 teaspoons baking soda
>   1/4 teaspoon salt

In another larger bowl, cream together in order until smooth:

>   1/2 cup softened butter
>   1/2 cup raw sugar
>   1 cup unsweetened and unsalted peanut butter
>   1/2 cup unsweetened applesauce (or pearsauce)
>   2 eggs

Gradually add dry ingredients to wet. Drop by teaspoonfuls onto cookie sheet. Flatten with a fork. You may want to rinse the fork in cold water periodically. It is also nice to dip the fork in raw sugar too, before flattening the cookie dough. Bake 350°F for 8-10 minutes.

Banana Chocolate Chip Cookies

These are Darci's favourite. Ahoy, Captain Darci!

In a large bowl, mix the following dry ingredients:

>1 cup brown rice flour (or white rice flour)
>1 teaspoon baking soda
>1/2 cup semi-sweet chocolate chips

In another large bowl, cream together:

>1/2 cup softened butter
>1/2 cup raw sugar
>2 small bananas (mashed with a fork)
>2 teaspoons vanilla

Then add, mixing well:

>2 eggs

Add the dry ingredients to the wet ingredients and stir until combined. Drop by teaspoonfuls onto cookie sheet. Bake at 350°F for 6-8 minutes.

Variations:

>Try pearsauce instead of bananas
>Try bananas and pecans
>Try coconut and bananas

Best Ever Ginger Snaps

Preheat your oven to 350°F. Get all your ingredients out including two large bowls and bake away. Makes about 36 yummy cookies.

In one bowl, mix:

>   3/4 cup white rice flour
>   3/4 cup tapioca flour
>   1/4 teaspoon salt
>   1 teaspoon cinnamon
>   1/2 teaspoon nutmeg
>   1/4 teaspoon ginger

In another bowl, cream together:

>   1/2 cup softened butter
>   1/2 cup raw sugar

Add:

>   1 egg
>   1/4 cup fancy molasses

Add dry ingredients to wet and stir until combined. Drop by teaspoonfuls onto a nonstick cookie sheet. Bake at 350°F for 8-10 minutes. Enjoy with a cup of tea at tea time with some friends .

My son likes to add currants. If you like, you may add a 1/2 cup to the dry ingredients.

Carob Pudding

In a large bowl, lightly beat and then set aside:

    2 egg whites

In a another large bowl, whisk together until smooth:

    $2/3$ cup carob powder (or cocoa)
    2 tablespoons tapioca flour
    $3/4$ cup potato milk, rice milk or soya milk

In a large saucepan, add:

    1 $1/2$ cups potato milk, rice milk or soya milk
    $1/4$ - $1/2$ cups raw sugar
    $1/8$ teaspoon salt

Mix well. Bring to a boil over medium heat, stirring constantly. Remove pan from heat.

Whisk carob mixture into hot milk. Bring to a boil over medium heat and boil for 2 minutes. Remove pan from heat.

Gradually whisk carob mixture into egg whites. Pour back into saucepan and cook over medium-low heat for 2 minutes. Do not boil. Add 1 teaspoon vanilla and pour into serving dishes.

Banana and Strawberry Shake
Recipe on page 15

Cinnamon Buns
Recipe on page 17

Cranberry and Banana Loaf
Recipe on page 18

Lemon Poppy Seed Loaf
Recipe on page 23

Pancakes
Recipe on page 24

Waffles
Recipe on page 27

Angel Food Cake
Recipe on page 31

Apple Streusel Coffee Cake
Recipe on page 32

Banana Chocolate Chip Muffins

Recipe on page 33

Carrot and Pineapple Muffins
Recipe on page 35

Cinnamon Pear Muffins

Recipe on page 36

White Cake

Recipe on page 41

Chocolate Chip Cookies
Recipe on page 51

Chocolate Hazelnut Biscotti
Recipe on page 53

Jam Cookies
Recipe on page 58

Pear Pie
Recipe on page 74

Chocolate Biscotti

In a large bowl, add the following ingredients and mix thoroughly:

$1/2$ cup white rice flour
$1/4$ cup tapioca flour
$1/4$ cup potato starch flour
1 $1/2$ tablespoons unsweetened cocoa powder
$1/3$ cup chopped hazelnuts
1 $1/2$ teaspoons baking powder
$1/4$ teaspoon salt

In another bowl, beat:

2 eggs
$1/3$ cup raw sugar
1 tablespoon hazelnut liqueur (optional)
    Frangelico® Hazelnut Liqueur is gluten-free

Add dry ingredients to wet, just until combined. Make two log shaped rolls on greased cookie sheet. Bake at 350°F for 15-20 minutes. Let cool on cookie sheet. Without removing, slice each log into $1/4$ inch thick slices and lay flat. Bake each side at 350°F for 5 minutes.

For those fancy occasions, place a thin layer of melted semi-sweet chocolate chips on cooled biscotti, then place in refrigerator until ready to serve. Gooey, gooey, good.

Chocolate Chip Brownies

My friend Jinny wanted to know if I had a brownie recipe. Of course I did. I gave her this one. Now she makes this brownie recipe all the time for her family and friends. They're fast, they're easy, and no one knows that they're gluten-free.

In a large bowl, sift together:

   1/4 cup white rice flour
   1/4 cup tapioca flour
   1/4 cup unsweetened cocoa powder (or carob powder)
   1 teaspoon baking powder
   1/4 teaspoon salt

Add:

   1/2 cup semi-sweet chocolate chips
      (or your preference, mine are dairy free)

In another large bowl, cream together:

   1/2 cup softened butter
   3/4 cup raw sugar

Then add:

   2 eggs
   2 teaspoons vanilla

Make sure this mixture is well blended before adding the dry ingredients. Stir in flour mixture just until moistened. Pour brownie batter into a greased 8 inch square pan. Bake at 350°F for 20-25 minutes. Frost with chocolate frosting when brownies are completely cooled, then sprinkle with a few chopped walnuts. Cut as desired. Serve to your best of friends.

Variations:
Pour batter into mini muffin tins and bake for 8-10 minutes. In October, use Halloween paper muffin cups for the liner and the kids will jump for joy. Well, maybe not for joy, but surely for a chocolate chip brownie.

Chocolate Chip Cookies

In a large bowl, combine the following:

> $1/2$ cup white rice flour
> $1/2$ cup brown rice flour
> 1 teaspoon baking soda
> $1/2$ teaspoon salt
> 1 cup semi-sweet chocolate chips
>   (usually semi-sweet chocolate has no dairy)

In another large bowl, cream together until smooth:

> $1/2$ cup softened butter
> $3/4$ cup raw sugar
> 2 teaspoons vanilla

Stir in:

> 2 eggs

Add dry ingredients to wet. Mix well. Drop by teaspoonfuls onto cookie sheet. Bake at 350°F for 8-10 minutes.

Variations:

> 1 cup unsweetened carob chips
>   (increase raw sugar by 1/4 cup)
> 1 cup sweetened carob chips
> $1/2$ cup coconut and $1/2$ cup chocolate chips
> $1/4$ cup coconut, $1/4$ cup chopped pecan nuts and
> $1/2$ cup chocolate chips

The combinations are endless. Experiment and Enjoy!

Chocolate Frosting

This frosting is well worth the extra effort.

In a saucepan, over medium heat, stir the following ingredients until the sugar and cocoa are completely dissolved.

$1/3$ cup water
$1/2$ cup raw sugar
$1/4$ cup unsweetened cocoa powder
pinch of salt

Turn the saucepan heat to low and, with an electric mixer, beat in:

1 egg white

(Please be very careful that the electrical cord is safely guarded.) Beat the frosting on high for about 8-10 minutes or until it becomes thick. Remove from heat and add 1 teaspoon of vanilla. Frost your favourite cake, muffin or brownie, or whatever your heart desires. Enjoy!

Chocolate Hazelnut Biscotti

There are two biscotti recipes because I couldn't decide which one was better. So I kept them both in the book. Enjoy them as we have.

In a large bowl, beat until frothy:

> 3 eggs
> $1/2$ cup raw sugar

In another bowl, combine the following:

> 1 cup brown rice flour
> $1/2$ cup chopped hazelnuts
> 2 teaspoons baking powder
> 2 tablespoons unsweetened cocoa powder
> $1/4$ teaspoon salt

Fold dry ingredients into egg mixture. On a greased cookie sheet, divide dough into 2 log shaped rolls. Bake at 350°F for 15-20 minutes. Let cool. On a diagonal, using a serrated knife cut rolls into $1/2$ inch slices. Lay flat side up. Bake each side 5 minutes. When completely cooled, spread each biscotti with the Chocolate Icing recipe found on page 54. Place in refrigerator until ready to serve.

Substitution:

> 2 tablespoons carob powder for cocoa powder

Chocolate Icing

This recipe is my favourite. It's great for soya ice cream, biscotti and brownies. If you want a thinner consistency, add more rice milk.

In a small saucepan, over low heat, melt gently:

1/4 cup semi-sweet chocolate chips (dairy free)
1/8 cup butter
1 tablespoon rice milk

Stir until smooth. Let stand for 5 minutes before using.

Christmas Sugar Cookies

These are always nice for a cookie exchange. They are simple, yet elegantly received.

In a small bowl, combine:

> 1 cup brown rice flour
> 1 1/2 teaspoons baking powder
> 1/4 teaspoon salt

In a large bowl, cream together:

> 1/2 cup softened butter
> 1/2 cup raw sugar

Then add, stirring together until smooth:

> 1 egg
> 2 teaspoons vanilla

Mix the dry ingredients with the wet until a nice dough forms in the bowl. Using a cookie press make your cookies according to the directions of the cookie press. I like the wreath shape. Sprinkle the cookie dough with red and green sprinkles, of course you need to check that they are gluten-free!
Bake at 375°F for 6-8 minutes.

Ginger Cookies

This recipe makes about 36, fast, easy and delicious cookies. Preheat oven to 325°F.

In a large bowl, mix well:

    1 1/2 cups brown rice flour
    1/2 teaspoon baking soda
    1/2 teaspoon ginger
    1/2 teaspoon cloves

In another large bowl, cream together:

    1/3 cup softened butter
    1/2 cup raw sugar
    4 tablespoons fancy molasses

Then add until well blended:

    2 eggs

Add the dry ingredients to the wet ingredients until just combined. Place teaspoonfuls of batter onto cookie sheet. Take a wet fork and dip it into a small bowl of raw sugar, press the fork gently on the cookies to make small indentations. Dip fork into sugar for each cookie or whenever needed. Make them small so you can just pop them in your mouth. Bake at 325°F for about 8-10 minutes.

Hazelnut Shortbread

These are especially fabulous around Christmas time.

In a large bowl, mix together:

   1 1/2 cups white rice flour
   1/3 cup ground hazelnuts

In another large bowl, cream together:

   1 cup softened butter
   1/2 cup raw sugar
   1/2 teaspoon vanilla
   Pinch of salt
   1 egg

Add the dry ingredients to the wet ingredients and stir until well combined. Divide the dough in half, placing each half on a sheet of wax paper. Using the wax paper, form the cookie dough into a nice round roll, about 1 inch in diameter. Chill for 30 minutes. Remove the wax paper and slice cookie dough into 1/4 inch thick slices. Place on cookie sheet and bake at 325°F for 8-10 minutes. Let cookies cool before removing them from the cookie sheet. Set them in a container in the refrigerator until ready to serve.

Jam Cookies

Simply lovely for tea time.

Warning - this is a double cookie recipe because they're so darn good.

In a large bowl, combine the following:

 1 1/2 cups brown rice flour
 1 1/4 cups tapioca flour
 1/4 teaspoon salt

In another large bowl, cream together:

 1 1/2 cups softened butter
 1/2 cup raw sugar

Then stir in:

 2 eggs
 2 teaspoons vanilla

Add flour mixture to egg mixture, mix well. Roll a teaspoonful of dough to make a ball in your hand. Then roll it in a small bowl of ground hazelnuts. Place on cookie sheet. Continue making small dough balls until dough is gone. Now press your thumb into the centre of the cookie ball and fill hole with raspberry jam or your favourite jam. Bake at 350°F for 8-10 minutes.

Lemon Pecan Biscotti

Absolutely fantastic with a cappuccino!

In a large bowl, sift together:

　　1/2 cup brown rice flour
　　1/2 cup tapioca flour
　　1 tablespoon baking powder
　　1 teaspoon salt

In another large bowl, cream together until fluffy:

　　1/2 cup softened butter
　　1/2 cup raw sugar
　　1 tablespoon grated lemon rind
　　1 teaspoon vanilla

Add:

　　2 eggs (beating well, one at a time)

Gradually add the dry ingredients to the wet. Then stir in:

　　1 cup chopped pecans

On a greased cookie sheet, divide the dough into 2 equal log shaped rolls. Bake at 350°F for 15-20 minutes. Let cool. Using a serrated knife cut the rolls on a diagonal into 1/2 inch slices. Lay flat side up. Bake each side for 5 minutes at 350°F.

Substitutions:

　　hazelnuts for pecans

Nutty Cookies

In a large bowl, combine the following:

> 1 cup white rice flour
> 1 cup ground hazelnuts
> 1 1/2 teaspoons baking powder
> 1/2 teaspoon salt

In another large bowl, cream together:

> 1/2 cup softened butter
> 3/4 cup raw sugar

Then add:

> 2 eggs
> 1 teaspoon vanilla

Set aside.

In a small saucepan, melt very slowly:

> 1/2 cup semi-sweet chocolate chips

Slightly cool the melted chocolate, then stir it quickly into the egg mixture. Now gradually add the dry ingredients to the wet ingredients. Roll onto a sheet of wax paper, using the wax paper to form a log, about 1 inch in diameter. Refrigerate for 30 minutes and slice into 1/4 inch cookies. Place on an ungreased cookie sheet and bake at 375°F for 6-8 minutes.

Peanut Butter Balls

The children will love these simple cookies, and so will the adults.

In a large bowl, cream together:

  1 cup unsweetened and unsalted peanut butter
  1/4 cup softened butter
  1 teaspoon vanilla
  1 teaspoon salt

Gradually add:

  1/4 cup brown rice syrup
  1/4 cup tapioca flour

Refrigerate for 30 minutes. Make 1 inch balls and place on cookie sheet, then back into the refrigerator. Now is a good time to make the melted chocolate, recipe below. When completed, dip one end of peanut butter ball into melted chocolate and place back onto cookie sheet. Refrigerate for 15 minutes. Keep cookies in a tightly sealed container in the refrigerator.

Substitutions:

  cashew butter for peanut butter

Melted chocolate

In a small saucepan, on low heat, add:

  1/4 cup semi-sweet chocolate chips
  3 tablespoons dairy free milk
  1 tablespoon butter

Stir until melted thoroughly.

Peanut Butter Cookies

In a small bowl stir together:

   1 cup brown rice flour (or white rice flour)
   1 teaspoon baking soda
   1/4 teaspoon salt

In a large bowl cream together:

   1/2 cup softened butter
   1/2 cup unsalted and unsweetened peanut butter
   3/4 cup raw sugar
   2 teaspoons vanilla

Then add:

   2 eggs

Make sure that all the wet ingredients are blended well together, now add the dry ingredients. Stir until smooth. Drop by teaspoonfuls on cookie sheet. Press each cookie lightly with a fork. You can also dip the fork into a small bowl of raw sugar to make sugar topped cookies. Top the cookies with a peanut. Bake at 350°F for 6-8 minutes.

Variations: Add the following to the dry ingredients

   1/2 cup semi-sweet chocolate chips or
   1/2 cup carob chips or
   1/2 cup coconut

Substitutions:

   cashew butter for peanut butter

Peanut Butter
Rice Crispies Squares

These squares were rated "great" by Joseph.

In a large saucepan, over low heat, stir until melted:

1 cup unsweetened and unsalted peanut butter
$1/2$ cup brown rice syrup
1 cup semi-sweet chocolate chips
$1/4$ teaspoon salt

Remove from heat and stir in:

1 teaspoon vanilla
3-4 cups brown rice crispies

Press into an 8 inch square pan. Let stand for 20 minutes in refrigerator and cut into squares. Fantastic every time.

Substitutions:

cashew butter for peanut butter
sweetened carob chips for semi-sweet chocolate chips

Strawberry Jam Squares

Coconut is one of those fruits that is either loved or not.
In my family it is well loved, thank goodness. I enjoy baking
these squares for my friends, especially those who love coconut.

Preheat oven to 350° F.

In a large bowl, cream together the following:

   1/4 cup softened butter
   1/4 cup raw sugar

Then add these ingredients, making sure to mix thoroughly:

   1 egg
   1/4 cup dairy free milk
   1 teaspoon vanilla

Now, to make the soft dough, add these dry ingredients:

   1/2 cup white rice flour
   2 teaspoons baking powder

Spread your dough in a greased, 8 inch square pan.

Measure:

   3/4 cup of strawberry jam and spread evenly on the
      soft dough

In another bowl beat together the topping:

   1/4 cup raw sugar
   1 egg
   1 cup unsweetened coconut

Smooth the topping on the strawberry jam. Lightly sprinkle
with raw sugar. Bake at 350°F for 15-20 minutes. When baking is complete, place pan under the broiler for 30 seconds to
brown the coconut. Let cool for 10 minutes before cutting
into squares.

Zucchini Cookies

I like these cookies especially for the kids as they do not know that they are nutritiously good for them. My one child hates zucchini. To this day, he has no idea that the cookies he gobbles up have zucchini in them.

In a large bowl, mix together:

3/4 cup brown rice flour
1/4 cup tapioca flour
1/4 cup potato starch flour
1/2 teaspoon salt
1/2 teaspoon baking soda
1 cup semi-sweet chocolate chips
1 cup unsweetened shredded coconut
2 cups shredded yellow or green zucchini,
    (leave the skin on)

In another large bowl, beat well:

1/2 cup melted butter
3/4 cup raw sugar
2 eggs
1 teaspoon vanilla
1/4 teaspoon nutmeg or cinnamon

Add the dry ingredients to the wet and stir just until combined. Drop teaspoonfuls of cookie dough onto a greased cookie sheet. Bake at 350°F for 12-15 minutes or until edge of cookie is lightly browned.

Substitutions:

1 cup of currants for semi-sweet chocolate chips.

Cobbler, Fruit Crisps, Pies, and Tarts

Blueberry and Raspberry Crisp

Variations are endless, this happens to be our favourite.

In a large bowl, combine:

> $1/2$ cup white rice flour
> $1/2$ cup raw sugar
> $1/2$ teaspoon cinnamon

Cut in with a pastry blender until crumbly:

> 5 tablespoons chilled butter

In a buttered baking dish, add:

> 2 cups of frozen or fresh blueberries
> 2 cups of frozen or fresh raspberries.

Top the berries with the crumb mixture. Bake at 350°F for 20 minutes or when the crumble is brown and the berries are bubbling through. Serve hot or cold. We love it both ways.

Note:

If using frozen berries, monitor your cooking time, as it may be longer.

Hazelnut Pie Crust

(makes 2 pie crusts)

In a large bowl, combine the following:

1 1/2 cups white rice flour
1/2 cup finely chopped hazelnuts
2 tablespoons raw sugar
1 teaspoon salt

Cut in:

2 tablespoons butter

Add:

3 teaspoons vegetable oil

Using a fork add:

about 1/2 cup cold water (until dough stays firmly together)

Place dough on a floured sheet of wax paper, sprinkle dough with more flour. Place another sheet of wax paper on top of dough. Using a rolling pin, roll dough out to the size of your pie plate. Remove top sheet of the wax paper. Now place your pie plate upside down on the exposed pie dough. Placing your hand under the bottom layer of wax paper, flip over pie plate and dough. Press dough firmly into pie plate and remove the top layer of wax paper. Trim edges with a knife. Fill with your favourite pie filling and enjoy!

Maple Walnut Tarts

These are totally delicious. You and your guests will be amazed.

Using the Pie Crust recipe found on page 75, measure and cut pastry into tiny tarts. Place into small muffin tins. The edges may become ruffled — not to worry, it adds to the look of the finished product.

Place 1/2 teaspoon of chopped walnuts into pastry shell.

Filling

In a large bowl, beat together:

> 3 eggs
> 1 cup maple syrup
> 2 tablespoons melted butter
> 1 teaspoon vanilla

Then stir in:

> 1 cup coarsely chopped walnuts (use pecans if you prefer)

Pour filling over walnuts in tart shells. Bake at 425°F for 12-15 minutes. Let sit for 5-10 minutes before removing your tarts from the tin.

I like little tarts, they are less messy, especially with children. In addition, they look more elegant when served with a plate of cookies for tea time.

Peach and Blueberry Cobbler

Simply divine!

In a large saucepan, combine:

>5 cups sliced peaches (peeled)
>1/4 cup raw sugar
>5 teaspoons tapioca flour
>1/2 teaspoon cinnamon

Cook slowly until mixture boils and thickens.

Then add, stirring gently and set aside:

>4 cups blueberries

Cobbler:

In a large bowl, combine with a pastry blender until crumbly:

>3/4 cup white rice flour
>1/4 cup tapioca flour
>1/4 cup potato starch flour
>1/4 cup raw sugar
>1 tablespoon baking powder
>1/2 teaspoon salt
>1/2 cup softened butter

Then add:

>1 cup potato milk (or any dairy free milk)
>1 teaspoon vanilla

Pour fruit mixture into a buttered baking dish. With a spoon, drop large spoonfuls of cobbler onto fruit mixture. Bake at 350°F for 20-25 minutes, or until fruit starts to bubble over the top. Serve warm.

Pear Crisp

This is truly one of our favourite desserts, especially when it is served with a scoop of rice or soya vanilla ice cream.

In a small bowl, combine the following using a pastry blender until it resembles crumbs:

$1/2$ cup white rice flour
$1/4$ cup softened butter
$1/4$ cup raw sugar
1 tablespoon maple syrup
$1/2$ teaspoon cinnamon
dash of salt

In a buttered baking dish, add:

5-6 peeled and sliced pears

Sprinkle the crisp on top of sliced pears. Bake at 350°F for 20-30 minutes. Ready when crisp is bubbling. Mmmmm- good!

Pear Pie

Pears are a wonderful alternative if you have allergies to apples. This is Joseph's favourite pie, Eli prefers pumpkin.

Prepare your pie crust using the recipe found on page 75.

In a large bowl, add:

> 7-8 peeled and sliced pears
> (I prefer Bartlett, but you may substitute with any type)
> 1/4 cup raw sugar
> 1/2 teaspoon cinnamon

Stir gently to evenly coat the pears. Place pears into prepared pie plate and dot with butter (I almost always forget this step). Place your second rolled pie crust on top of pears. Trim the edges and pinch together. Make slits on top of pie. Bake at 350°F for 45 minutes or until you see bubbles through the vents.

Pie Crust

I love this recipe, and so does everyone I have served it to. Someone always remarks on how lovely the pastry tastes. Are they saying that to be polite? You try it and let me know what your friends say.

In an extra large bowl, blend together:

> 4 cups white rice flour or brown rice flour
> 1 cup tapioca flour
> 1/2 cup soya flour
> 4 tablespoons raw sugar
> 1 teaspoon salt

Cut in with pastry blender until crumbly, then set aside:

> 1 package of vegetable shortening or pure lard

In a 1 cup measuring cup, add:

> 1 egg   1 tablespoon rice vinegar

Beat egg and vinegar together.

Fill measuring cup with cold water to measure 1 cup. Stir.

Pour egg mixture into flour. Blend until well combined. This recipe makes 6 single pie crusts. Use immediately, or wrap individually with wax paper and place in freezer until needed.

When you are ready to prepare your pie, remove pie dough from freezer and allow to thaw at room temperature. Place dough on a floured sheet of wax paper, sprinkle dough with more flour. Place another sheet of wax paper on top of dough. Using a rolling pin, roll dough out to the size of your pie plate. Remove top sheet of the wax paper. Now place your pie plate upside down on the exposed pie dough. Placing your hand under the bottom layer of wax paper, flip over pie plate and dough. Press dough firmly into pie plate and remove the top layer of wax paper. Trim edges with a knife. Fill with your favourite pie filling and enjoy!

Pumpkin Pie

This is Eli's favourite pie. I bake it all year long as we can never wait for Thanksgiving. I always double this recipe and make two pumpkin pies.

Crust:

Follow Pie Crust recipe on page 75. Brush the fluted edges with a little egg to prevent the crust from burning.

In a large bowl, combine the following ingredients:

> one 14 oz. can pure pumpkin
> 2 beaten eggs
> 1/2 cup raw sugar
> 1 teaspoon cinnamon
> 1/2 teaspoon nutmeg
> 1/4 teaspoon ginger
> 1/4 teaspoon salt

Gradually stir in:

> 1 cup vanilla rice milk

Pour into unbaked pie shell. Bake at 425°F for 15 minutes, then reduce the heat to 350°F and continue baking for another 30 minutes, or until knife or toothpick comes out clean.

Main Dishes, Sauces and Side Dishes

After School Pizza

Using plain rice cakes, place four on a cookie sheet. Top each rice cake with the following ingredients or your choice:

- 1 tablespoon ketchup (gluten-free)
- 1-2 tablespoons rice mozzarella cheese
- 4 slices pepperoni (gluten-free)
- a few slices of olives
- sprinkle with Italian seasoning

Broil in oven for less than a minute, or until cheese is melted. Let cool slightly, then serve to your kids for after school snacks. Fantastic!

Basil and Parsley Oil Sauce

It's fast, it's easy and it's tasty.

In a small frying pan, sauté:

    3 tablespoons olive oil
    1 teaspoon basil
    2 tablespoons chopped parsley
    4-6 minced cloves of garlic
    a sprinkle of cayenne pepper.

Sauté on low heat for 3-5 minutes. Toss with cooked rice pasta and top with Romano Cheese. Serve hot.

Note:

My children can tolerate Romano cheese as it is made from sheep's milk. You can check at your local food store for Romano cheese made with rice milk if you prefer.

Fast Tomato Sauce

This is my Mom's recipe. Thanks Mom!

In a medium size saucepan sauté:

    2 tablespoons olive oil
    1 finely chopped cooking onion
    1 teaspoon Italian seasoning
    1 teaspoon basil
    2 tablespoons chopped parsley
    1/4 cup chopped red pepper (optional)

Sauté until onion is opaque, 2-3 minutes.

Add:

    one 8 oz. can purée tomatoes
    4 oz. of water
    1 peeled carrot
    1 celery stalk
    dash of salt and pepper
    pinch of raw sugar

Cover and let simmer for 45 minutes - 1 hour. Cook rice pasta as usual and top with tomato sauce. Sprinkle with Romano cheese. We love our Romano cheese!

Variation:

Add lean turkey sausage to sauce (frozen or thawed, I've done it both ways) but remember to cook this sauce for at least 3 hours.

Fish Batter

Andrew, Eli, and Joseph love to fish, so I had to come up with a batter that complimented the catch of the day. And I did. The following recipe has been modified from my friend Alice's recipe. It's perfect every time.

In a large bowl, mix together:

   1 cup white rice flour
   1 teaspoon salt
   1/4 teaspoon pepper (my men love their pepper)

In another bowl, beat together:

   2 egg yolks
   1 tablespoon softened butter
   3/4 cup beer (gluten-free)

Add the dry ingredients to the wet and stir until well combined. Set aside.

In a small bowl, beat until stiff:

   2 egg whites

Fold egg whites into batter 3-4 times. Now dip your fish fillets into batter, one piece at a time, and sauté in a hot pan with 1/2 inch of vegetable oil.

You will love this recipe. We catch perch all summer long and never tire of eating it with this batter. It is light and fluffy, and sometimes tastes like potato chips.

Substitutions:

   water for beer

Lasagna

Use the Fast Tomato Sauce recipe, found on page 81.

If you prefer to eat the vegetables in the lasagna, then chop the carrot and celery before adding them to the sauce.

While the sauce is cooking, grate your rice mozzarella cheese and cook your rice lasagna noodles. When noodles are almost cooked, drain the water and rinse in cold water. Let stand until your sauce is complete. When your sauce is ready:

1) Add a couple of spoonfuls of sauce onto the bottom of a lasagna size tray. (9" x 12")
2) Add your first layer of noodles. You may find that it has fallen apart; don't worry — patch it as you would do with a puzzle. The end result will be the same.
3) Add another layer of sauce evenly over noodles.
4) Liberally sprinkle your rice mozzarella cheese.
5) Sprinkle Romano cheese. You may want to eliminate this step if you can't tolerate sheep milk.
6) Another layer of rice noodles.
7) Continue to repeat the same process as above. Make sure you end with cheese on the top.
8) Cover and seal lasagna tray with a sheet of tin foil. Bake at 350°F for 45 minutes or until you see the sauce is boiling. Remove the sheet of tin foil and bake for another 5-10 minutes.
9) Remove from oven and serve hot.

You will find the effort was well worth it. I tend to make this for Sunday dinner. If by chance I have leftovers, which is usually never, I like to store it in the freezer or keep it for leftovers the next day. Or why not double the recipe and make two? I served 4 trays of lasagna for our boys' First Communion, and no one noticed that I used rice pasta or rice mozzarella. It was well received and well worth the effort.

Nacho Chips

My children could not eat corn for awhile. I made these chips from rice sheets purchased at a local health food store.

First place about 2 rice sheets on a cookie tray topped with water. Let stand until completely soft. Remove from water, pat dry and cut into eight triangles; like a pizza. Place triangles into a hot frying pan with 1 inch of hot vegetable oil. Remove when crisp. Lay chips on a paper towel to remove excess oil. Sprinkle with salt and serve with salsa.

Nokedli

Nokedli are small flour dumplings that can be made with a spaetzle maker. It is a Hungarian dish that my friend Janice, served for supper one night. Since then I have been making it gluten-free. After making this dish, I'm sure you will agree with me that the spaetzle maker is one of the necessary kitchen gadgets for the gluten-free kitchen. It costs about $8.00.

In a large bowl, stir the following:

  2 cups white rice flour
  1/2 cup potato starch flour
  2 eggs
  1 cup cold water
  1/2 teaspoon salt

Bring a large pot of water to a boil. Rest the spaetzle across the pot, fill it with a cup of dough and slide the handle back and forth, making sure the dumplings fall into the boiling water. Repeat until all the batter has been used. Serve it with your favourite stew or add some spaghetti sauce. Simply marvelous darling!

Pizza Night Pizza

Every Friday night we have pizza and a movie. The following is my favourite pizza dough recipe. Enjoy it with your family and friends as we do every Friday night.

Place the following ingredients into the baking pan of your bread maker:

   1 cup of water
   1 tablespoon softened butter
   1 tablespoon raw sugar
   1 teaspoon salt
   1 3/4 cups white rice flour
   1/2 cup potato starch flour
   2 teaspoons yeast

Place baking pan back into bread machine and select dough setting. When the cycle is complete spread pizza dough onto a greased 12 inch pizza pan. Add your favourite tomato sauce, top with grated rice mozzarella cheese, chopped broccoli, chopped red pepper, and chopped green onion then sprinkle with Romano cheese. Place pizza in a 350°F oven for 15-20 minutes or until the bottom of the pizza is brown.

Stuffed Zucchini

Slice 2 zucchinis in half lengthwise. Core out a little bit of the seeds and stuff with the following:

In a small bowl, combine the following until bread crumbs are wet:

- $1/2$ cup bread crumbs (this can be made from rice crackers or stale left-over rice bread chopped finely in a blender)
- 1 teaspoon olive oil
- 1 tablespoon chopped fresh parsley
- 1 clove finely chopped garlic
- salt and pepper to taste

Use more olive oil if a wetter stuffing is desired. Spread on halved zucchini and bake in a covered casserole dish. Bake at 350°F for 1 hour.

Vegetable Stir Fry

As with any stir fry, I use whatever I have in the refrigerator. The vegetables may differ, but the sauce always stays the same. You may add any or all of the following vegetables in any quantity you desire. I never measure my vegetables, as I always use up what I have on hand.

Heat your large frying pan and add:

    2 -3 tablespoons olive oil
    beans
    snow peas
    chopped celery
    diced red pepper
    sliced yellow pepper
    diced zucchini (and you thought I would leave zucchini out)
    chopped broccoli
    1 clove minced garlic
    2 diced small onions

When vegetables are almost done, add the following and sauté until the liquid thickens.

    $1/4$ cup water
    1 tablespoon tapioca flour
    1 tablespoon peanut butter
    2 tablespoons soya sauce

Serve vegetables over a bed of brown rice or add your favourite cooked chicken, turkey, or beef. Voilà, the perfect meal, in my opinion.

Zucchini Patties or Cheese Patties

(as my children call them)

My mother-in-law introduced this recipe to us. I changed it somewhat to accommodate our diet. Thanks Ardith.

These are fantastic as a main course or side dish. We also like them cold the next day.

In a large bowl, combine the following ingredients:

    2 cups grated zucchini
    $1/2$ cup grated rice mozzarella cheese
    $1/2$ cup grated rice cheddar cheese
    $1/2$ cup white rice flour
    2-4 cloves garlic (I prefer 4-6)
    4 eggs
    salt and pepper to taste

Heat a frying pan or a nonstick skillet and spray with cooking oil. Place a tablespoonful of batter in pan and cook until firm around the edges. Flip over and cook the other side. Serve hot.

Index

C